THE BOOK OF FORTUNE

Books by Daniel Mark Epstein

YOUNG MEN'S GOLD (1978)

THE FOLLIES (1977)

NO VACANCIES IN HELL (1973)

POEMS BY DANIEL MARK EPSTEIN

THE
BOOK
OF
FORTUNE

THE OVERLOOK PRESS/WOODSTOCK, NEW YORK

First published in 1982 by
The Overlook Press
Lewis Hollow Road
Woodstock, New York 12498

Library of Congress Cataloging in Publication Data

Epstein, Daniel Mark.
    The book of fortune.

    I. Title.
PS3555.P65B6   811′.54   81-18907
ISBN 0-87951-146-X   AACR2
ISNB 0-87951-151-6 (deluxe)
ISBN 0-87951-152-4 (paper)

Printed in the USA

The poems in this collection first appeared in the following magazines:

The American Scholar: "Mannequins," "Miami," "Climbing." *The Kenyon Review:* "Ode To Virgil." *The Michigan Quarterly:* "Fortune." *The New Republic:* "Easter." *The New Yorker:* "The Sentry of Portoferraio." *Occident:* "Portrait of the Photographer." *Poetry Miscellany:* "Letter to Thomas Edison." *The Smith:* "Notes For a Conversation With My Grandfather." *The Virginia Quarterly Review:* "Lafayette Square." The author is indebted to *The Journals of John Burroughs* for images and phrases in "Letter to Thomas Edison."

CONTENTS

CLIMBING

When he gave up mountains he became
a window washer, hoisting himself on block and tackle
fifty stories above the street. For the love of heaven
    is an addiction like stealing
fast time from the round jail of the clock.

He loves high windows. Saves them for last,
looking down on the traffic, crawling workers
whose vision he rinses clean as fresh glass.
Pigeons swing like puppet birds under his hands.
        But does he think downward?

Does he love his fear of the lurking flaw
    in the scaffold, the crack in a faithless plank?
Does he think of the fatal journey
        between his living and his death? No.
He looks in on the nodding accountants, winks

at an astonished secretary who drops her file.
He looks out along miles of reflected rooftops,
    the sky mirrored in the invisible window.
It is like flying on the surface of our lust
    for a visible horizon.

By noon the top windows are clear as a sudden answer,
      at dusk pure gold,
by night they are pure moon blue.
Sadly he rides the elevator down
and starts again at the foot of the blind wall.

THE SENTRY OF PORTOFERRAIO

Blame this island town for the broken boy
who keeps his watch high on the falcon fortress.
Blame this town of rose and sea-green stone
stairways, and the daredevil swallows.
Was it not enough that beneath a circus of birds
his eyes should blindly fix upon each other?
Born lame as an old joke
did he have to grow up in such a town
of pinnacles, one cocked leg
cursing the steps that lead him to his home?

Accuse the snake in the cactus, fig, and grape
gathering liquor from the rainless air;
scold fish heads in the monger's stall,
cats on the sill. Charge the parents
of sturdy children whose eyes renew the horizon,
whose legs conquer mountains and pines.
Did we not conspire in narrow prayers
to divide his share of health among us?
Did we not invest in our cross-eyed sentry
suffering enough to make a nation wise?

It is the fury of providence
to crowd a family of pain into one creature,
then crown him guardian angel of a town.
It is his lonely insistence on Heaven
that leads lovers to the sudden view
of their bodies broken beautifully against themselves,
that leads our village skyward to command
an ocean, rise and stand up to the sun!
But somebody has to pay for the hobbling climb,
somebody has to pay for his double vision.

PORTRAIT OF THE PHOTOGRAPHER

You are in control of the machine.
Driving East from California in three days,
rigged to the steering wheel, accelerator
and brake by pullies,
tendons of wire and stainless steel.
I drag you from the car like a sack of kindling.

Long ago I told the story of your flight
from the window in San Francisco, back
when drugs were cheaper, the living high and fast;
made what myth of it I could in our defense.
Telling the tragedy once is enough, like living it.
Wasted pain to go over it all again.

Eleven years after that fall you come
to see me in this ground floor lounge
the Church provides us for a studio
because you couldn't make it up my stairs.
I wheel you down the hall, half air, half fire.
No body, but the camera screwed to your chair,

prosthetic, gleaming, formidable,
fashioned for the hand that cannot move
quick as the eye, the starved hand
with no animation nearer than the elbow
to turn the dials and trip the shutter.
No body but the camera! Between us

after fifteen years of love there is
neither distance nor time,
and only flesh enough to make appearances.
Each time I see you seems to be the last,
and so it should always be, with friends.
You tell me you hold on to us like death,

and the camera, commanding "Face the window.
Stretch out on the sofa, hand on your cheek.
Close your eyes. Now open them." So you have
pursued me, shooting away on foot and on wheels
for more than half my life, convinced
there must be something worth preserving.

The room sails into a shadow. You ask me
to look out and give you a reading on the sun.
A low cloud bank, heavy, slowing down.
Gold border turns to purple, then to black.
Not much time. You burrow under the hood.
Focus. My life flickers against the lens.

You slap the negative in, cover the barrel,
then doff the lens cap softly so not to shake
the camera, the furniture, the light.
And maybe this time
if we do not perish first, maybe this second
if we can hold perfectly still

maybe this time, surely by now you have died
enough to take me for what I am
and I can look like the man I have become.

MANNEQUINS

This indecent procession of the undead
invades the Avenue windows, dressed to kill,
sporting tomorrow's clothes and yesterday's faces.

One struts in a velvet shaft of midnight blue,
slashed down the back in a diamond heat of lust,
gold crown at the wrist and throat, a garnet ring.
Here Lucie Anne side-slits a terry dress
trimmed in Venetian lace
and petal edging on the camisole. There a lady
most unladylike, lounges
in silk of liquidly drapable muscadine,
grinning the wine-red of wickedness. Another
borrows the schoolgirl's kiss, the cupie bow,
eyes round and empty as pots, and the apple cheek.
For we also yearn to join the innocent in their clothes:
Jill in her jumper, Johnnie in his jeans,
sheep in their fleece, the pig in his narrow poke.

But I prefer them naked, the posturing frauds,
free from any trace of shame, and without nipples
or the fur that friction-proofs our parts for love.

I like them headless, oh Marie Antoinette,
       what beauty knocked in the executioner's bucket!
I like them wigless, as a rack of bullets.
I like when a leg is kicked out of its socket
or an arm flings back in some preposterous gesture
as if to say
"So happy to have missed the agony of meeting you,"
or
"We who are early salute you from the backs of our heads."
I love when the feet swivel for a fast retreat,
and the head jerks in wonder defying the neck.

But when they are assembled and decked out,
they turn vicious, whispering through the glass:
"How have you achieved your shabbiness?
Where is your glamour, the youth you were born with?
Where, if you have one eye, is the other,
and if you have three limbs, where is the fourth?
Where is your hair, marcelled or carefully windblown,
your eyebrows, the artfully painted lips?
Put your face to the glass, you wretched snail,
kiss me, you desecration of a man."

MIAMI

After years of stock-car racing, running
rifles to Cuba, money from Rio, high
diving from helicopters into the Gulf;
after a life at gunpoint, on a dare,
my father can't make the flight out of Miami.

Turbojets roar and sing, the ground crew
scatters out of the shadow of the plane.
My father undoes his seat belt, makes his way
up the aisle, dead-white and sweating,
ducks out the hatchway, mumbling
luggage was left at the dock, his watch
in the diner. Head down
he lurches through the accordion boarding tube,
strides the shining wing of the airport, past
windows full of planes and sky, past bars,
candy machines and posters for Broadway shows.
Gasping in the stratosphere of terror, he
bursts through the glass doors and runs
to a little garden near the rental cars.
He sits among the oleanders and palms.

It started with the Bay Bridge.
He couldn't take that steel vault into the blue
above the blue, so much horizon!
Then it was the road itself, the rise and fall,
the continual blind curve.
He hired a chauffeur, he took the train.
Then it was hotels, so many rooms
the same, he had to sleep with the light on.
His courage has shrunk to the size of a windowbox.

Father who scared the witches and vampires
from my childhood closets, father
who walked before me like a hero's shield
through neighborhoods where hoodlums honed their knives
on concrete, where nerve was law,
who will drive you home from Miami?
You're broke and I'm a thousand miles away
with frightened children of my own.
Who will rescue you from the garden
where jets flash like swords above your head?

EASTER

Spring, when the evil of the world
          dresses with a whore's flamboyance,
japonica, forsythia fountain the red and gold
of Hell. My grandmother thrashes in the madhouse,
a great beauty in a jungle of screams.

Medicine tricked her in here. Now only pain
can set her free. It must be the pain,
          whipping those miraculous cheeks
pink and fresh as a girl's. From the torment
of drug withdrawal she has returned, wasted,
to the angelic figure of an ancient child.

If only she were as easily comforted!
A child cries in the night, you switch on a lamp
and the terrors fade like morning stars.
But at noon my grandmother's cell
is a hazard of devils
and the drug of light has lost its power.

She's afraid the priest might hear her bargaining
          with some chiropractor of evil
to yank the pitiless kinks out of her spine.
A long life of begging for the longer life
of her spirit, and it has come to this!
She'd junk it for a single night of rest.
She waves away the holy bread and wine,
for there's no more hunger to feed her suffering.

NOTES FOR A CONVERSATION
WITH MY GRANDFATHER

Nothing but prophecy seems fair,
for the inequity of our separate knowledges
hurts most. I'll come as I am,
a portrait the artist left to chance:
my mouth and hands done justice maybe,
but the eyes and brow a glance and wrinkle shy
of full expression. You are entire,
yet I must face you half made-up,
younger than you were when I was born.

I see you milling in the garden
like St. Francis. Birds and poverty.
I see you stripping the backbone from a fish.
You are floating on a suitcase
in the North Atlantic, riding the whirlpool
over your torpedoed steamer. Shipwrecked
again off the coast of Argentina,
you comb the beach six months,
go begging, carry water for the whores.
You rise from the black ground of photographs,
young rake with derby cocked, propped on a cane,
a plump and laughing girl on your free arm.

Once you drove me through a twilight
landscape December had beaten flat,
to the clearing where a giant holly
fountained berries, held them in spiny leaves
against the sky. A lonely God!
What were you hunting when you found Him there?

Summer, you would gather figs on the bank
of the black and knotted Nanticoke
River you swam at dawn
for twenty years, to keep the body young.
The brown fruit split under your thumb.
Pink meat shone through seed clouds
and clear honey.
                You lived on air
while holding the fig open for me to enter—

but all this history is out of place.
I meant these words to sound on a live ear.
I'll settle my debts on all experience
in the currency of a plan
or closely figured prophecy.
Maybe we can still meet equally,
as two portraits ruined: yours, a masterpiece
worn by wind and sun;
mine scarred by the painter's rage
for what was promised yet could not be done.

Make my memory as faithful as these plans.
I will be strong. I will be rich
if the world holds,
tell the truth as long as the Truth holds,
love men and women as I have loved you.
Beyond such certainties I will live in the cold
mystery where both of us will die.

Now I am ready to go to you, ready
to pour this wine of our shared harvest. . .
But why am I wavering in the door?
Can I still be wondering if all these words
aren't pilfered? Have I borrowed what is left
of your life and bought another rag
to keep me warm? Why am I shuddering?
Afraid of what the family might think?
What will your daughter, my mother say
if she hears me at your bedside whispering
these love words
as if this were a wedding night?
The boy is selfish, rash and rude
to make this show, this mockery of our grief!
He thinks he's greater than the dying man.

I don't. They never knew my mind.
But someone does. A harsh, all-seeing light
rushes, crowds your room as if the sun
had risen on both sides of us at once.

Daylight without shadow, more terrible than night!
Whatever words I may find fit for me
are too poor to stand in such a light.
I'll keep those promises to myself,
memory, apology and plan,
not out of some shame or grief,
despair or doubt you would understand.

I'll keep this to myself because it is poor
and nothing short of glory would suffice.

As I enter your room I will be silent
as we imagine the near room to be
awaiting you. Silent
as the crashing wave, the blasted oak
lightning loved and entered
when there were none to witness, none to hear.

SCHOOLHOUSES

The staircases are always last to go,
winding into the sky like cries of defiance
against the wrecking ball and dynamite.
And the "up" staircase is still adamantly "up"
though bells are silenced and the rushing students
have all passed on, and "down" is "down" although
there are no more classes above or below.
No matter. Imagination, delighting in space
as does memory, climbs and runs downstairs
stopping to rest at a landing, take in the view
that finally escaped the narrow windows.
It whispers: In this room I learned
numbers refer not to things but to what we think
about things, and down that hall
I fell in love for the first and longest time.
Here I discovered uranium. There, an honest man.
Here I learned the shortest distance between two points
is sleep. There I learned I would die, but not when.

Before the school was leveled it was abandoned
and served as an altar
where the neighborhood children celebrated
their rage against learning. My daughter and I
used to go walking there
to check on the vandals' progress,
windows newly smashed, legends of graffiti,
chairs dismembered, the clock with twisted hands,
books read by rain and fire, their spines crushed.
There is no vandalism so inspired, none so pure
as children's rage against what has loved
and failed them. It is a bitterness of heart.

I want my daughter to see the school
as mortal, nothing like a church.
I came upon one chapel in the woods,
abandoned but intact, the steeple
piercing an overhanging bough,
wrens in the belfry, the rose window
casting its roulette of sunshine
over the scattered pews. And in cities
where the Church has long ceased to serve
the parish they will sometimes comfort the ruin,
board up windows where stained glass was stolen,
consecrate the door with a wreath on Christmas.
Teenagers sneak into the nave, to make love
or drink wine in the enduring sanctuary.
But the school is mortal. Vandals sentence it
and wreckers come to carry out their will.

Now the low cedars press against the wind
in a field that was once schoolyard
and my daughter clings to my hand.
She doesn't know where we are. She
is afraid I am telling the truth:
the school *was* here that now is gone,
and home, bed, mother, father,
are equally frail and liable to disappear.
We circle the site and I am pointing
and explaining—rubble, rubble—
wondering whose locker held the bomb.

How many teachers slept with Valery Strauss?
What are the prime numbers after ninety-seven?
Why is the school more eloquent in this state
than it was in its stern glory when we were young?
And why couldn't the vandals have been entrusted
with the wrecking of the schoolhouse? That
would have been more practical, more humane.
Are they too anarchic to do the job right?
Is it the nature of vandals that
they cannot deliver what they advertise?
The original Vandals were passionate and thorough.
I read about them in Ancient History.
They overran Gaul, Spain, and North Africa,
invaded Italy and sacked Rome destroying
many monuments of art and literature.
The schoolhouse vandals are sneaky, picayune,
anonymous, unworthy of their name.

Why do I take such joy in leading my daughter
on the outskirts of this animated emptiness?
What have I learned in school but the savage joy
of asking questions that brought the building down?
Why have I had to grow old to ask such a question
as why do we have to grow old to become wise?
I suppose I would rather be young and foolish
and probably am, though you'd never know it
to see my grey hair. Joy made me grey.

LAFAYETTE SQUARE

The certificate of Coroner Patterson
in the case of Mrs. Henry Adams, who died suddenly
in this city on Sunday last, is to the effect that she
came to her death through an overdose of potassium
cyanide, administered by herself. She was just
recovering from a long illness, and had been suffering
from mental depression. She left no children."
                    —*The Washington Critic*
                    December 9, 1885

Who is it on the stair, who in the hall?
My hemisphere, the master of the house.
More flowers! All the porcelain, love,
is choked with purple iris and carnations—
you garland my room as if I were a corpse.
Did you startle me? Like a baited chain
of mousetraps, my nerves go off at a hair's fall.
You might have tiptoed in on a down cloud
(as you seem to do), your breath hushed,
and still slammed my soul in terror between
the bedroom door and the broken window of my heart,
out of which flies, what? My thought
in letter-winged shape of a white dove.

What was I writing? Oh nothing. What sort
of nothing needs to hide itself from my husband?
Just a note to my sister, news of the day.
"Elms bend with wet snow along a street
mobbed with foreigners rushing on
preposterous errands, Patagonian trade,
treaties, hawking foghorns and elixirs.

The house we are building is almost done.
From my creaking balcony next door
I trap it in my camera: the gargoyle drains,
the corner turret scanning the White House.
Our great lawmakers lodged across the Square
trample on the Mormons and Chinese.
Blaine is called up, Shipherd testifies.
Madame Catalano sails away
to Russia Wednesday next with three
babies, an alligator, a wolfhound.
I have all this by hearsay,
augury and my window's parallax.
For we are declining the circuit of winter teas.
I don't go out. I won't go out at all."

I was about to add:
"Through all the hours of sorrow, my husband
stands like an arch-angel at my side,
riposting harpies with a paper knife."
Thus I would lie for you, though no one
will ever know the true range of your kindness.
You are the gentle hand holding
the knife to my throat.
Why do you snatch it away?
Now you've scattered the pages on the floor,
go on and read the first lie of the day
in my letter's true address, "Dear Father."

Why do I write to my father, why
should I lie to you, my husband? You shine
your pitiless study lamp into my mind,
plot the navigation of my blood,
tide and wind, my calm and rising gale.
It was only last April that the doctor died
who was my father, and my fever began to rage,
the sickness that is grief unmoved by prayer.
No mother to share my sorrow, none to remember,
no child to nurse and laugh away despair—
Why shouldn't I write to him? The words are mine.
Our Sunday letters held me in his world,
whether I journeyed to hell or Washington.
And who is more distant than the newly dead,
more starved for comfort, love words in the dark?
You, my husband, you, my inquisitor.
Does your jealousy reach into his grave?
I think that he is more alive than you.

And if he's not. Why shouldn't I address the dead?
It is the house profession, the house passion,
your weird Confucian necrology,
stuffing your presidential ancestry
with feathers of shredded fact, excelsior.
My husband is the son of a great house,
the house of Adam, fathers of the tribe
of Adams, unfallen Adams all.

My husband is the end of perfect breeding,
thought out of action, action ended,
the begonia flowering out of a wheatfield.
My husband is the mortician of his clan.
You cram them to the lips and prop them up,
President, Grand-President, Senator,
for all the world as if they were alive.
So they are more alive than you and I
who live across from the ancestral home,
spectral saboteurs of the White House.

Forgive me love. It is the sickness, sickness
of grief and loneliness. He was all
the father and mother I had. Where are my children?
Was there no more room in history
for children? Oh I have heard you mourn
our fated incapacity to bear
another Adam or a dewy Eve,
a child for your knee, another President.
But how does it happen, love, in some
naked space dreamed high above the bed,
or breathing the common air, sharing a thought?
Ideas never made a child, though they kill men.

Forgive me, love, it is the sickness
of December, and loneliness, and irony.
What comfort can you afford, try as you may?

You whisper to my sadness: "All of life
is nothing but a series of farewells.
The bitterest is spoken. Look to the future."
Then you rise, kick open the study door
on such a howling multiverse of dragons
no monk in guilt's traction could conceive:
"A million homicidal engineers
running an ungodly godlike train
a hundred million horsepower full speed
up and down the shrinking landscape.
Space deranged by electricity, horsepower
doubling every fifteen years, the days
of time are numbered in a meteor world
where Rome will no longer be Rome, nor time time.
We are the slaves of coal, die with our master.
Apocalypse by law of logarithms. New York a nest
of twenty million insects in the throes
of metamorphosis, changing worms to wings—"
Enough! Just leave the future to itself!
Must the historian turn to prophecy? Help!
First you drive me into my father's arms,
then you cite your revelation
that when the body's broken, content spills
into a maze of branching rivulets,
a vapour of quick rainbows in the blue,
a few drops in the reservoir of truth.
Not even my father's ghost can hear me now!
What consolation in your nightmare future
if it is not "Better to be dead?"
Let me follow my father. You live on.

You say I cannot die, "for we are one."
And you have hidden from me, half in jest,
every pointed object in the house,
knives honed for vengeance by the Japanese,
your razor blade, the ivory-handled cutlery.
Your irony is under lock and key
with dueling pistols rusted impotent,
or disguised as an obsequious compassion.
Am I chained to the pleasure of your company?
What am I to you, your wife,
an image at the banquet table's end,
the hostess schooled in fashionable wit,
companion on horseback, partner in despair?
And more than this, when all the guests are gone:
mother, sister, cradle, sepulchre,
repository of such terror and remorse
as only an infant of two hundred years
could know and bawl out in the nursery.
This and more than this. We are not one,
but you have lived within me, crowded
precious space I needed for my soul,
lived within me, not in the happy way
of man in woman, the circle of her arms,
to die bodily then rise in love again.
You have fattened in me like
a foetus satisfied to live unborn
in the body of a virgin. I
was the woman you could never be,
nor can I, for the goddess will explode
the strongest temple men can shut her in.

The house we are building is almost done.
From my balcony I've watched it rise
out of the mud, on the backs of laborers
shouldering mortar hods, sinews of brick
to launch in double arches for the portals.
The architect has taught you Romanesque.
Sometimes I think the soul of it is dust
as brick powder sifts into my room
tincturing the windowpane.
Sometimes I think the house is history meant
to be seen from afar, never lived in,
a foursquare, window-slotted monument
three stories high with a turret at the quoin.
I will not live there though it's built for me.
But I have kept a record of the house
in photographs with the tripod camera
you gave me to keep my mind out of the past.
Here is the vacant lot, here is the canyon
delved and blasted out of Lafayette Square.
Here is the first story. Scantlings
of white pine sketch out the halls
of the second story you shall walk alone,
bedroom, dressing room, a suite for guests,
all flooded with skylight, without the walls.
Here you are wrangling with Richardson
whether the parlor window should look out
street-level, or pitch above the roof
of our neighbors across the way,
over the White House toward the whiter sky.

Here is the sea-green, onyx chimney piece.
We wanted purple African porphyry
(a stray vein runs from Braintree to Lynn
under Boston harbor,
diamond-hard, a curse to the quarrymen.)
It was too dear, though nothing be too dear,
and the Mexican onyx glowed so exquisitely
it made your soul yearn, you wrote to me
in the North, while I watched my father die.

So here is the history of our home
from mud to sky,
cobweb of running beams and crossing planks,
the naked corner and the standing wall.
A miracle, this little box, a time machine
where a slide coated in silver collodion
is struck eternal witness to the light.
The camera masters time! In nitrate
solution, silver and the fixative
potassium cyanide, so deadly some say
three drops in a cup of tea will heat
one's blood to gall and paralyze the heart.

I have planned a portrait of myself
to keep you company when I am indisposed,
so wan and winter-pale
the light cuts through me to the world beyond.
You will forgive me if it is not drawn
as Whistler would have me, or your friend

St. Gaudens might cast his American saint
in the light of science, or as virgin chained
somewhere between the portal and the shrine.
We want something more gothic about the house.
South of the weathervane cocked for a May wind,
north of the red chimney there will break
through solid beam and attic tile and slate,
a slender tower sprung from a broken arch,
unbuttressed, aiming at the infinite.
From the crown of that tower, in full view
of all the capital, I'll wave goodbye...

Go on your stroll without me, and forget
all this, forgive my winter weariness,
my anger and my love if it proves cruel.
Solstice cautions the daylight and I weep
for the absence winter glorifies to a season,
glazing nature, widowing the world.
Leave me to my work, my solitude.
The picture will be waiting when you return.

LETTER TO THOMAS EDISON
FROM JOHN BURROUGHS

T

O THOMAS EDISON, MENLO PARK, NEW JERSEY

April 21, 1916

Dear Thomas,
         As you brought light into the world
let me call the sound of April into your silence,
for April is in heat and pairing with the sun
         in my vineyard.
Meadowlark on the hickory, his high note flies
         like the shaft from a crossbow.
Bobolink's in the hill meadow singing of boyhood.
Surely birds were hatched in a human heart
         for the bluebird warbles of home, the catbird pride,
and my red-eyed vireo preaches peace of mind.
Oh the triumph of a robin, faith of the sparrow!
A sheaf of reedy willow-brook notes
         the red-winged blackbirds play
in orchards piled to the clouds with apple-bloom.
Under-hill the highhole calls, voice from the soul
         of April, the new furrow, seed and the planting.
Bees hum, the air is strung with a resonant chord.

Highhole calls again from the currant patch:
Go and spade horseradish, spinach
and melting roots of parsnip. Let us taste the soil!
Earth is ripe for the plough, it lusts for it.
I mark out the grape trenches, open furrows
         for young vines. I guide the team of horses.

Make room for my vineyard, dig out place-rock
                where it peeks from the turf.
We break the stoney sleep of ages
with bars and wedges probing, with dynamite blasting.
Where no sun has shone in a million years
                we let it in,
and sometimes we find green lichen in buried stone.
O life will work in the merest crack or chink!
Twilight, and I am glowing head to foot,
                fresh from the earth-bath.
In every cell of my brain I feel the land
        newly plowed. The furrow has struck in
and sunlight has photographed it on my soul.

Now my landscape floats into the sky, my cup
                brims, the horizon swims with divine elixir.
The walls of my self are glass. I see through pores of my skin.
Laws of nature joining the part to the whole,
the holy nerves of the universe are laid open
like a spider web glossed with dew and morning light.
My thoughts go scratch with hens in the dry leaves,
        with geese nipping spears of grass.
My thoughts fly north with ducks migrating,
        hover about the farm and garden fires.
They career away to the sugar maple woods
        where sap is clinking slowly in tin buckets.
Man is a pace of earth and a rag of sky
                and laws of the outer world are born in him.

Forgive me, friend, I wander from pure music
    to pure thought, where I have no license,
and such thoughts need no cracked horn to trumpet them.
They are the inward coda of our age.
I had to live seventy years to see such a Spring!
To see it, Thomas, not that it wasn't there
inside me, the calendar furled in a catkin.

Which leads to my greater purpose. Could there be
something greater than playing Nature's phonograph
for the Wizard of Menlo Park, the music lover
who can't hear the robin's racket, the blackbirds jangling?
Yes! For you read my letters and books, you
who do not need them, whose soul is so high-domed
it spans my hillocks, and the mountains and seas.
Adam never walked in so rich a garden.
It is not for you, but for our mutual friend
I mimic the meadowlark and the highhole.
I write you what I fear he'll never read
because he is restless, worse than deaf and blind.
I write you what Henry Ford will not hear from me.

Remember our last excursion, the caravan
            of millionaires gone vagabond under my wing,
Ford, Firestone, and I, your faithful guide,
            naming birds and leaves, reading the stars,
leading our motorcade through the Adirondacks.

Somewhere near Vermont a car broke down.
When the village mechanic blamed the motor,
Henry coughed and tipped his battered derby.
"I am Henry Ford," he said. "I say
this motor is running perfectly." The rustic paled.
He said, "Well, then the electric spark has failed."
"I am Thomas Edison," you growled.
"I say there is nothing wrong with the wiring."
The mechanic looked to heaven, then to me,
my laughing, wrinkled cheeks, my beard of snow,
and said "I suppose this must be Santa Claus!"

And so I do remain to Henry Ford:
Saint John, kind John, bird man of the Catskills,
fit to name the beasts as Adam, and as innocent.
"Bring John along and leave the books at home,"
he says and then kidnaps me from the farm.
Don't get me wrong. You know I love the man,
    the fire of his will, his diamond pride.
But I fear for him as I would for my own son
if he seemed so ill-equipped to die.
You might say it were well enough to be equipped
        to live, at Ford's age. So would I
if it were enough for the man to live for himself.
But you who shed your light upon so many
        know the inventor lives not for himself
but for the inheritors of what he finds.
Such living wants a sense of death as well,
        and Henry doesn't see that he will die.

Tell us the symptoms of his malady,
        case history and prognosis, Dr. Burroughs!
A farmboy in love with birds and plough horses
        gets lost in a busted watch and wanders
for days among twirling gears and spiral springs.
By the time he finds his way back to the world
        the lark has grown a pulsating halo
of functional definition, the lark lives
                to keep the greedy locust from the corn.
Rivers that once ran only to dazzle him
                now bend to nurse the pasture,
seeds are to split, and sprouts to branch and blossom,
flowers to lure the bee making liquor of light.
The waterpump is seven times more beautiful
        than idle rainbows haunting the fans of spray.
Handle finds its door, lock finds its key,
                sunup, sundown, moon and tide and wind
likewise learn their places and their uses.
Father, mother, autumn, clock and chime
                forge their ineluctable chains of music,
rapid and passionate as the boy's heart.
On his mother's death he writes this elegy:
"The house is like a watch missing its mainspring."
Here's less than Truth and more than Poetry!
Henry sees himself as a cocked piston,
        discrete, at the heart of a fabulous machine
that might run smoothly through the universe
                making us kind and clean and prosperous
if only the parts would let him assemble them.

He moved from watch to clock, from the clock case
to the booming chambers of a steam engine,
from steam to gas that fueled his motorcar,
from car to factory. There every man
played his part, turning creation into fate,
an empire of spidery banging Model-T's
cast in Ford's image, burning the roads of America.

Where did we last see him? On the deck
of the S.S. *Oscar*, the "Peace Ship" bound for Norway
that Henry chartered out of pocket
"to bring the boys home from the trenches by Christmas."
Wilson couldn't, nor could Sir Edward Grey,
but Ford with his cargo of crackpots and one idea
would stop it. "Money lenders made the war.
Sell tractors instead of guns and they'll come home."
A band played drums and brasses above the crowd
that waved handkerchiefs and wept and cheered.
Some leapt into the water, and some sang,
and Ford, throwing roses from the rail,
offered you a "million" if you'd go. You didn't hear.

He's home now, blaming the newspapers and Jews.
War goes on, the Kaiser wants the sea and land.
Henry wants to run for President.
President! He cannot name five Presidents!
The father of so much power in the world,
looks on history like his bastard son,
a shabby accident, an old disgrace,
the best-forgotten folly of his youth.

His present eclipses all our past. Yet
what is power? Did you think Niagara Falls
crashing through daylight, a great display?
What lies silent in the earth around,
of which Niagara only whispers a phrase?
Power is gravity claiming its own,
the lust of rain to blend with sea again.
Man sets his oaken wheel between two waves
and gravity mulls his wheat. All life
and movement is in breaking the equilibrium.
But, from drop to wave to paddle wheel and mill,
all things are an arch and every rising stone
is a keystone. One cannot move a single stone
without the risk of bringing the building down.

Talk to him, Thomas. He'll listen to you.
I show him a waterfall and he builds a plant.
I show him the birds of the Everglades
and he returns from Europe with a shrieking cage
of songbirds to set loose in America:
rare parakeets and Moorish nightingales,
birds that scarce could live where they were born.
Tell the man his head is full of birds,
his heart a spring chorus if he would listen!
You are his hero, his idol, the only one
in whom he sees himself as more himself
than he is, one in whom he sees
his own green thoughts and instincts ripened,
full grapes on your vine, rounded in sunlight.
He sees you in himself. I hope he's right.

When I think how different my light could have been,
your light, that warms my page after sundown
     and makes the night my study!
I wonder if the bulb you made would shine
        the same if you had been a different man.
Would it sweep the shadows from the rafter cracks
     and corners if you had not known
some child might need the comfort of light there?
Would it spark the wrinkles of my brain
     with morning wakefulness had you not known
daylight never sleeps in the human mind?
Suppose you had been a bitter, sullen man,
        a hermit or churl. You might have made
light that rides only the surface of things,
     fit to find our way from room to room
but not to trace the corridors of thought
where humor slaps its thigh or revery sees
      tide rip the winter waves to ragged foam.
You saw how daylight bronzes naked skin, then shines
    right through the skull to blood and bones and heart.
You took no model but the sun, made light
      to heal and pray by, light to make love by.
Mimic only the sun, my children. And like him
     grow larger at thy setting!
Man's triumph comes in the way of Nature's will.
      She calls to him:
"My horses are flying this way, vault into the saddle
     and ride along or be trampled if you fall.
My steam will ferry you and your household
     around the globe if you can harness it,
or rend you to atoms if you miss your hold.

My streams will saw your lumber, grind your wheat
    or grind you if you lose the upper hand."
Man appeared and man will disappear, time
        squanders him recklessly as autumn leaves.
What could nature care when it is her own
        coffers death enriches, what can she care
if we are all blown back to the sun and stars?

Think of all Ford has done, what he might do,
        and you and I in our graves.
He made a motorcar. Well enough!
It is a blind and desperate thing
        ready to roll in a ditch or climb a tree.
Could he have built the machine with more sympathy?
Yesterday I came from driving my son to the station.
I aimed my new Ford at the old barn
door. Then I got rattled, the car ran wild,
burst through barnside with a splintering crash
        of boards and timbers, cats and chickens crazed.
Rolling to the cliff's edge, the flywheel caught
        on a rock that took more pity on me
or I would have landed on the other side of Jordan.
Thus fear delivers us to the thing we fear.
I knew it would happen. Talk to him, Thomas.
He may make a machine
        to transport us from New York to Baltimore

or this world to the next by distillation
        of bodies into the soul's electric charge.
All well enough! Bravo! First make him see
        the universe that is one human soul
            lest the future traveller
arrive without his proper past, his father's wish,
        the rainbow's logic, and his mother's pride.

Jubilee of goldfinches in the elms. They come
        every spring to these trees on the same day
as if by harmony of common mind.
They invade the vineyards and the garden
        for green seeds of chickweed,
they attack the shut dandelions,
                they feed on hatching elmseeds
                        rifling the winged disk of its germ.
No bird has so pretty a way of match-making, they join
        in singing each other's praises.
What is their song? Of luminous greenness everywhere
        as leaves let the light shine through.
For nature is young, we can see the blood in her veins,
        her skin is so delicate and thin.
Morning is a pale youth, a nude maiden
        veiled by her own hair.
O the shy blossom of hazel and butternut
        and the river shimmering through green mist!
New time always, the verge of time, the days turning
        their beautiful sad faces toward us.

The days are children. We have them a little while
        and then they are taken from us.
Mossy boulder, milk of the black birch,
        scent of meadow rue and ginger-root
with dusky floral bell, white trillium.
If fortune filled only the measure of man's dream
        we should all be buried in debt.
If I think my will is free, that's good enough!

Skylark climbs in a spiral wing-song, trailing
        sparks of melody, crowns his flight
with ecstatic trills against the brilliant sky.
The best time is coming, time to make sacred in passing,
time of the greatest milk yield, succulent grass,
        clover fresh in the fields and sweet syringa
about the house, and daisies and buttercups.
Scent of blooming rye fields and wild grape
and the calmer song of birds, their first madness
        and lovemaking over.

Come Thomas, leave your shop while we have time
and let's take to the open road for the strawberry days!

ODE TO VIRGIL

1

Astral mechanic! Forcaster of empires! Vergilius!
The children of Europe are gathering under your stars.
They throng the dialectical Squares and Roundabouts.
They are marching through medieval walls and streets
under flags all the colors of your far-flung planets.
The children of Europe are marching into the constellation
        of Orion
under the blue flag of morning, marching under red flags
into their parents' bedrooms at the instant of conception,
marching under black flags into the death camps!
They are cracking the armored seed of history, storming
your citadels in divine frenzy, like locomotive sunflowers.

Children of Berlin drive the Mercedes through a wall
of political graffiti, swasticas, hammers, multi-lingual
        sexual puns,
the blue children of Prague weep into the crockery.
The children of Paris cry all the way to the altar,
children of Belgrade ball into the mouths of cannon,
the children of Berlin cry all the way to the bank.

They are mourning the death of Marx who died
from turning over too many times in his grave.
Red flags at half-mast flutter on the slack lanyards.
They are mourning the deaths of Locke and Rousseau
who died of cancer, flaking away in golden parchments.
Their blue flags mirror stars half-mast in heaven,
white flags flame to black tatters.

The children of Europe are striking, Virgil
and Rome is paralyzed. Nothing works.
The docks are striking, and airplanes and freight-trains,
gears are locked, the dynamos freeze, the piston sticks.
The gas and electric are striking
and the mail and the refrigerators and televisions.
The Gypsies are striking in the Piazza Navona,
their children have been starving for centuries,
the whores are striking on the Via Veneto,
everybody is lying down on the job.
There is a general strike and there are all the little strikes.
I myself am striking in self-defense.
Vergilius Maro, this is your American correspondent in Rome,
Date line Friday, April 14, 1978, submitted not only with
due respect, but the utmost admiration.

2

Praise Vergilius, patron saint of Ford and Edison,
for he built a bridge of air that would take him anywhere
and spun from silver a mirror that could see
a distance of seven days journey, intrigues and traitors.
Good work Vergilius! The art of sorcery is in a sorry decline!
What sports car will hold the roads
that tunnel our psychic ocean, span the mountains of the sky?
What T.V. news broadcast can bring us tomorrow?

Praise Vergilius the seismograph, his brass archer
stood in the herb garden at Monte Vergine
with drawn bow threatening Vesuvius;
praise the prophylactic insecticide, the brazen fly
by mathematical art disposed in a gateway,
which kept a plague of flies from the city of Naples!
Praise the father of Frigidaire and packaged foods,
whose market kept meat fresh 500 years.

Praise Vergilius, rake and cocksman
for he fell in love with Nero's daughter
who invited him up to her tower in a basket
at midnight, then left him dangling in mid-air
for all the folks of Rome to see at dawn.
Praise Vergilius, master of revenge, for in his rage
he put out the fires of Rome
and made the citizens kindle their torches one by one
on her nude body bent dog-fashion in the Forum.

Praise Vergilius, father of public works and central intelligence,
for he devised the Salvatio Romae, palace of bronze
to house a delegation of graven heralds.
When a province revolted its mannequin rang a bell,
the bronze horseman atop the palace shook his spear
and aimed it at the province in revolt.
Praise Vergilius the prophet who claimed his security system
would last until a virgin should bear a child.

3

Pneumatic sage, son of the Empire, come home!
Your villa is on fire! Vergilius, all is forgiven!
St. Paul regrets you died too soon to be converted.
He was looking for you all over the Compagna.
Deep underground your specter sat at a table
piled high with books, meditating under two candles.
Our lean Saint entered the cave mouth, when
thunderclap, copper archers shot out the lights
and sage and study fell to ashes.

Vergilius, your children are burning, crossing the streets
under red flags against red lights.
They love red the color of rage and fire and blood,
as they love the crucifixion and ritual murder.
They love red the apple and red the devil and red the dress,
red the mouth and red the threshold of twilight.
Traffic snarls in the Piazza Venezia. Down with Mussolini!
they cry, fifty years too late. Machine guns
bristle around parliament because your children
have taken to kidnapping the ancient senators.
They are following your stars, Vergilius,
because that's the way you left them.

Snow in Madrid, Franco haunts the bullring
like a castrated matador.
Fog in Paris, De Gaulle's tenacious ghost
is kicking calcified shit in the Bastille.
Is this your terrible beauty, Father William?
A plastic restoration of Cologne as real as life
with a scarred Cathedral for reproach?
Churches survive but what god will survive the churches?
How can a poor traveller think with all this racket?

Hush children, America is sleeping, her sun
lags half a day behind. Sweet dreams, America!
Hush children and hear the story of an orphan
adopted, buried and raised by the kind magician.

FORTUNE

(Imitated from Villon)

Famous sages called me Lady Luck
in better days. Now who are you to cry
and call me killer, you nobody knows?
I've seen better men hauling slag at foundaries
and chipping stone from caves for a dog's wage.
So what if you live in squalor, does it
give you the right to bitch and moan at me?
You're not alone. Pipe down and count the dead
I cut off in their prime before you were born.
You aren't a ragged patch on a hero's ass
so sit down and shut up, take it
from me and roll with the punches, Dan.

Think of the proud Kings that I've cut down!
I butchered Priam. There was no tower so
high I couldn't reach him, no castle wall
so thick I couldn't break its back.
What about the elephant-jockey Hannibal?
Death caught him in Carthage. Remember Scipio
got his, though he died old. I sold
Caesar in the Senate, ruined Pompey
in Egypt. I sent Jason down to rest
with the fishes. Hell, I once set
the whole town of Rome ablaze. Take it
from me, things could be much worse for you, Dan.

Bloody Alexander would have scaled
the Pleiades or any cataract aimed at heaven.
Rat poison got him. King Arphaxad,
I crushed him on his banner like a gnat.
I put Holofernes to sleep, the pagan oaf,
so Judith could steal his dagger, cut him off.
What about Absalom? I snatched him naked
and hung him from the clouds as he tried to run.
Robespierre tried the rusted Guillotine
after a thousand heads had dulled the blade.
I can dish it out, and you can take it
from me, Dan, and take it as it comes.

Now listen, Fortune talks once to a man:
I don't mean you any special harm.
But if I had my way and didn't need a God
of Paradise to work my will I wouldn't leave
a crumb for your plate or rag to keep you warm
and I'd magnify by ten your every pain.
Count your lucky stars before they run
against you, while your eyes can see them, Dan.